CUSTODY OF THE EYES

Anthony Giardina

BROADWAY PLAY PUBLISHING INC
New York
www.broadwayplaypublishing.com
info@broadwayplaypublishing.com

CUSTODY OF THE EYES
© Copyright 2008 by Anthony Giardina

Cover photo by Roger Mastroianni
First printing: February 2008
I S B N: 978-0-88145-362-1
Book design: Marie Donovan
Word processing: Microsoft Word
Typographic controls: Ventura Publisher
Typeface: Palatino
Printed and bound in the U S A

CUSTODY OF THE EYES was first produced at the
Cleveland Playhouse (Michael Bloom, Artistic Director;
Dean R Gladden, Managing Director), with the first
public performance on 28 April 2006. The cast and
creative contributors were:

DONALD LEGER . . . . .J R Horne
ROBERT SULLIVAN . . . . .Kenneth Tigar
EDMOND LEBLANC . . . . .Joseph Collins
SHEILA ROSENTHAL . . . . .Jan Leslie Harding
MRS CALLAHAN . . . . Paula Duesing
RILEY ROSENTHAL . . . . Alexander Timothy Biats
GARY BURGER/FERRYMAN . . . . Mark Mayo

Director . . . . Michael Butler
Scenic design . . . . Russell Parkman
Costume design . . . . .Charlotte Yetman
Lighting design . . . . Nancy Schertler
Sound design . . . . .James C Swonger
Stage manager . . . . .John Godbout
Casting . . . . .Elissa Myers & Paul Fouquet

CHARACTERS & SETTING

DONALD LEGER, *sixties, Bishop of a Diocese in Maine*

ROBERT SULLIVAN, *sixties, formerly a parish priest, currently a Brother in a Benedictine monastery*

EDMOND LEBLANC, *early thirties, parish priest*

SHEILA ROSENTHAL, *early forties, member of Father LEBLANC's congregation*

MRS CALLAHAN, *late sixties-early seventies, Father LEBLANC's clerical assistant*

RILEY ROSENTHAL, *eleven,* SHEILA's *son*

GARY BURGER, *early forties, pediatric nurse*

FERRYMAN, *to be played by the same actor playing* GARY

The play takes place in various locations on an island off the coast of Maine, on the ferry connecting the island to the mainland, and in the garden of a Benedictine monastery in rural Maine. The time is the recent past, soon after the sexual abuse troubles in the Catholic Church.

for Doug Hughes

ACT ONE

Scene One

(A ferry)

(The set should consist of a central bench, or two chairs, behind which an altar rises. For the ferry scenes, the altar should be disguised to resemble the bridge of a boat. Before the bench, separating the set from the audience, is a rope, meant to represent the rope guarding the ferry from the dock. To one side, stage right, a ship's hold, which can be lifted, later, to reveal a plot of earth. Above the altar, a screen should be hung, on which images can be projected. [The author's suggestions for the set are meant to serve only as a blueprint. For instance, no screens were used in the Cleveland Playhouse production.])

(For the ferry scenes, the mast of a freight boat. Stage left, two chairs and a table, which serve, on the ferry, as seats and a simple flat surface.)

(At the top, FATHER EDMOND LEBLANC *faces us. He is in his early thirties, not classically good looking but attractive, not least because he doesn't know this about himself. He is wearing the traditional black suit and collar. A suitcase is beside him. He's cold, and holds his collar closed. He speaks directly to the audience.)*

EDMOND: A nun. I must have been six, seven, in Catechism class, preparing for Holy Communion. Terrified by the mysteries. A nun. Tried to explain the origin of the separation of the angelic host. I say "tried",

but she didn't merely "try". She spoke as if it were cast
in stone.

God sat the angels down, she said. There was only
heaven, no hell. Only angels. No devils. Sit down,
God said, I'm going to pass a picture around. It was a
picture of an infant. All the angels, in their turn, looked.

And then God said, Raise your hand if you can love
this—baby—as you love me.

So. Half the angels raised their hands, the other half
kept theirs down.

A chasm opened. The naysayers plunged into a pit
of fire. Those who had raised their hands— *(He lifts his
arms, gently, to indicate ascension.)* What I love about this
story is that its absolutely true. Something is handed
to us. We raise our hands or not. There is no second
chance. Not really *(Beat)* What the nun added was, the
fire never really hurts those in hell. They're numb to it.

But they have to constantly relive the unmade
gesture. In hell, their hands are constantly being raised
to an imaginary, unseen being. If I had only—known—
that I was being tested. I would have—.

*(Beat. EDMOND starts to raise his hand. Ferry's horn blows.
EDMOND lowers his hand, removes his collar, stares at it a
moment before throwing it into the sea. He watches it float
by, then quickly exits.)*

*(As EDMOND exits, two priests come forward, also holding
suitcases. They enter and sit on the bench. Both men are in
their early sixties. One is dressed in a monk's robes, the other
in street clothes, but wearing a clerical collar. They are
BISHOP DONALD LEGER and FATHER ROBERT SULLIVAN,
hereafter referred to as DON and BOB.)*

*(A FERRYMAN follows them and proceeds to the front of the
stage, holding a rope [separate from the one guarding the
ferry]. He casts it off. Sound of the ferry taking off. The
FERRYMAN passes the priests on his way into the boat,
but offers no acknowledgement.)*

DON: *(After the* FERRYMAN *exits, almost secretive)* You see that?

*(*BOB *offers only a questioning look in response.)*

DON: No acknowledgement. Not so much as a nod to us. Could who we are be any clearer?

*(*DON *adjusts his collar.* BOB *takes a moment to consider* DON's *collar, his own robes.)*

BOB: I don't think so, no. I'd say we scream priest.

DON: And this is a—what did you call it?

BOB: A freight boat.

DON: Smells like the dickens. Not even the proper ferry.

BOB: It was full.

DON: They could have fit us on. Once upon a time, and not very long ago, the waves would have parted. "Save a seat for you, Father, on the foredeck?" They'd have been honored to have us. A *bishop,* no less. *Drinks* would have been offered.

*(*BOB *only looks at him, slightly dumbfounded.)*

DON: What are you looking at?

BOB: I'm wondering how out of touch a human being can be.

DON: You're referring to our recent "troubles". Why do you suppose I decided to come on this little investigation? I could have sent someone else. Don't hide! I said to myself. Go and do your job just as if nothing had happened. One of our shepherds has strayed and I'm going to investigate what went wrong.

BOB: Bully, Donald. But don't expect the ferry system to pin a medal on you. Just be grateful that the worst we're getting here is indifference.

DON: Indifference to the Church is a cover. You ask me, that whole scandal just gave people a further excuse to stay away. God leaves the equation, though they know God's always there. They *know*. They don't *want* Him there, it makes life too *difficult*, so seeing us as bad men, as a bunch of child molesters and liars, is their way of salving their consciences for having turned away from a God who's still very much *there*. *(Beat. He's pleased by this.)* Watch.

(DON stands, stretches, moves toward the rope and begins to play with it, finally unhitching it altogether, at which point the FERRYMAN *from the top of the play appears.)*

FERRYMAN: Don't touch that, Father.

DON: *(Putting it back)* Sorry.

(The FERRYMAN *disappears, at which point* DON *allows his delight to show.)*

DON: What'd I tell you? There's your evidence right there. That man we believed was so indifferent, he's been eye-balling us all along. We fascinate them.

BOB: It's actually quite dangerous.

DON: What is?

BOB: That rope is the only thing separating us from—

(DON looks over the edge.)

DON: Yes. I take your point. *(A shift of mood now. He stares at the water thinking about something and experiencing a kind of empathic terror. Then he forces his gaze away.)* It's supposed to be a pretty island? This ghost island?

(BOB offers an unknowing stare in response.)

DON: You visited him there, this priest who took off—the architect of this whole mess—this young Father Leblanc?

BOB: I didn't. No. He came to me.

DON: Traveled all the way to your monastery, did he?
Under duress, was it? To seek advice from his old
confessor? Could you have stopped this terrible thing
that happened?

(Beat. No answer from BOB)

DON: Well, we have business to attend to on this island,
yes. Get to the bottom of this. But there's no reason we
shouldn't also— *(A look of pleasure)* Sightsee. I took the
opportunity— *(He goes to his suitcase, unzips it, removes
a paperback guidebook.)* —to have Lavelle from the
Chancery pick this up for me. A guidebook to the
islands. This one only merits a couple of pages. Still.
Points of interest. Forgive me, Father, I don't get out.
Walk. I'd like to walk. One of the perils of my position
is that I am always eating. Going from place to place—
this one's celebration, the Knights of Columbus dinner,
the Boy Scout Jamboree—

BOB: *(A thrust he can't resist)* Still invited there, are you?

DON: Still invited. Yes.

*(*BOB, *amused, takes out a pair of obviously expensive
sunglasses.)*

DON: Those designer glasses, are they?

BOB: They are.

DON: Can I— *(Meaning "see them?")*

*(*BOB *hands them over.)*

DON: Must have cost a pretty penny. Thought you
had to give everything away when you entered the
monastery?

BOB: I did. You could say I went on a little spending
spree before I entered.

DON: That's what got you into trouble, wasn't it—
your free-spending largesse?

BOB: Not the money, no. It was never the money.

DON: Still, you're well rid of it. What you've got now,
splendid. No longer a parish priest but a Benedictine
monk. I was *distressed* to receive your letter saying
you're not—happy—there.

BOB: Yes, I would have thought you were quite thrilled
to have me out of your Diocese.

DON: I am no such thing.

BOB: One less offender to worry about.

DON: I took no pleasure in your disgrace.

BOB: *(Taking him at his word, but carefully)* Well, I have
come to wonder whether I didn't accept that disgrace
too readily. After much thought, whether I didn't give
in too easily to what was a spurious charge to begin
with.

DON: *(Cagy around this subject)* Ah.

BOB: Were my timing not so unfortunate, I might ask to
come back, Donald. Still, I would like to discuss what
might still be possible. Within these new limits.

DON: *(An unreadable reaction)* Well, yes. Yes. We've
plenty of time for that. That's one of the reasons I
brought you, Robert. To discuss that request. But first
things first. You knew this boy. Let's get to his story.
This young unfortunate priest's awful story.

BOB: I thought we might first discuss my—

DON: *(Cutting him off)* The story, Robert.

BOB: *(keenly aware of how the direction of the conversation
has been subverted)* He came to me. Last Fall.

*(A ship's horn, and a shift of light to the ship's hold. From
out of his suitcase, BOB, in darkness, removes a straw hat.
Puts it on. At the rear of the stage, he finds a hoe. Lifting the
hold compartment, he uncovers a plot of earth. We are in:)*

Scene Two

(A monastery garden)

(On the screen above the set, the image of trees)

*(BOB gets down on his knees, does some simple hand
weeding. Then he stands and hoes the ground. He stares
into the sun. It's hot. He does not enjoy this work, but goes
back to it. After a bit, he removes, from out of the folds of his
robe, a small transistor radio. Fiddles with it until he can find
classical music playing scratchily. He places the radio near
him.)*

*(EDMOND enters, unseen . He watches BOB a while,
saddened, as if he is watching a man in a fallen condition.
Finally, he breaks in.)*

EDMOND: Father.

BOB: *(Turning. Surprised, delighted, but a subtle man.)* Son.

EDMOND: *(An old joke between them)* Holy Ghost.

(A warmth, suppressed, between them.)

BOB: *(Leaning on his hoe. Where to go first?)* You catch me
in turnip season.

EDMOND: A tasteless, unnutritious vegetable. Why do
you grow it?

BOB: *(briefly overcome)* You know vegetables now, do
you? The boy who once didn't know how to open a can.
What change is this? *(His manner is noticeably gayer in
EDMOND's presence than it has been in DON's. He gestures
now with his hand, asking EDMOND a question.)* How did

you get here? Haven't you been assigned to some
remote island?

EDMOND: I drove. Caught the early ferry. I am lucky
enough to have a priest visiting. Foreign. Irish. He said
the eight o'clock. The last ferry back leaves at nine
tonight. So I have— *(Checks his watch)* —five hours,
if I'm going to make it.

BOB: We usually like to be warned when an extra guest
is here for lunch. You might have called.

EDMOND: I don't have to eat. Or—in town, I noticed
a lunch spot. Can you leave?

BOB: Of course I can This is not prison, Edmond.
*(He makes a face allowing that yes, it is. Then, picking
up on* EDMOND's *unasked question:)* Yes. Say it.

EDMOND: I can't quite—get over the change.

BOB: It must seem a great comedown. You're used
to seeing me in flowing robes, at the head of a
congregation. Spearheading the building drive.
But there is no barbed wire strapped to my thigh,
I assure you. And this is not my grave I'm digging.
We can press flesh.

(They embrace. Something awkward on EDMOND's *part.)*

BOB: See? Nothing happened.

EDMOND: *(Embarrassed)* I didn't—

BOB: Oh, you did. Fear is written all over your face.

*(*EDMOND *shakes his head, not wanting to go where* BOB *is
leading.)*

BOB: Edmond, loosen up. Please. I am not an entirely
different person, not a reprobate. I have had a disgrace,
that's all. I chose to come here. *(Beat)* Look. You didn't
drive four hours, leaving your flock to a possibly

seditious Irishman, just to visit your old confessor,
did you?

EDMOND: No. That should have been the cause.
I should have come before now.

(BOB *waits for more.*)

EDMOND: I'm considering a fall of my own, Father.
That is to say—. (*He tries to smile, to minimize this, but can
neither finish his whole sentence or hold his gaze on* BOB.)

(*On* BOB's *face, meanwhile, a curious mixture of sadness and
concern. When* EDMOND *doesn't seem to be able to go on:*)

BOB: That is to say what, Edmond? Have I been waiting
for this? I snuck into one of your early sermons, after
your first assignment. You told a story about going for
a swim and a steam at the local health club. The steam—
well, you were going after some sort of metaphor—
(*Gestures to indicate how little he cares for that type of
sermon*) All I could think was, no, no, don't go there.
You're a young, good looking man addressing a
congregation of credulous females, don't give them an
image of your own nakedness, they'll never be able to
replace it with God.

EDMOND: I'm too autobiographical, I know. Things
happen to me, I don't know where else to look for
images. But it's not that.

(BOB *looks relieved for a moment.*)

BOB: Then it's only a question of faith. I am so relieved.
I thought you were getting laid. (*He touches his heart.*)
Look, about faith. Go easy on yourself. Very few of us
have it.

(EDMOND *looks at him a certain way, as if this is a familiar
tease.*)

EDMOND: We can go away? Talk?

BOB: Here. Perfect silence. What we're famous for.

(EDMOND *listens, realizing that this is in fact true. After a
moment, he gets down on his knees. Something in his face,
profound.* BOB *watches him, at first frightened, then
half-annoyed, half-amused.*)

BOB: Oh, get up. Please. I could never tolerate your
intensity when you were a student. I can't tolerate it
now.

EDMOND: I thought I would confess.

BOB: No. Talk to me like a man. It is a woman, isn't it?

EDMOND: *(Reluctant, standing)* It is a woman. But it isn't
what you think.

BOB: No. It never is.

EDMOND: *(A sudden flare-up)* Why does everything have
to be reduced to the sexual? As if there can be nothing
else driving us? There are other things. Other things—
(Coming to himself; embarrassed) Forgive me. I lose my
temper. But this is not—the common disgrace.

BOB: Then?

EDMOND: Father, an embarrassingly naked question:
who are we? Our role is what—exactly? Why does the
world need us, not to mention individual members of
the congregation—?

BOB: Edmond, you're going to have to talk in specifics.

EDMOND: A woman came to me last Fall.

(*As* EDMOND *speaks the last line, another shift of light,
this time onto the altar area. Projected onto the screen: a
cross.* EDMOND *immediately crosses to the altar area, just as*
MRS CALLAHAN, *a widow in her seventies, enters and says
her first line. There should be a seamless transition into:*)

Scene Three

(The church)

MRS CALLAHAN: Father, a woman here to see you..

(EDMOND looks at her: what can she possibly mean? As if, for the moment, he's lost the simple meaning of words.)

MRS CALLAHAN: You made an appointment. She says. She didn't go through me.

EDMOND: A woman? To see me? Well— *(Of course it's all right. No big deal. He's even glad.)*

(SHEILA enters. She is in her early forties, formerly close to a beauty. Life's done a bit of a number on her. If there's any way to convey she's dressed differently for this meeting than for other, similarly formal meetings, do so. A skirt, stockings, good shoes, not comfortably worn. Something covering her head.)

SHEILA: If it's not good, I can come back.

EDMOND: Nonsense. No. Did we speak?

SHEILA: I made an appointment with someone.

(There's an awkwardness to the scene. Neither knows quite how to proceed.)

MRS CALLAHAN: You're all right, then?

EDMOND: *(Called to himself)* Yes. Of course.

MRS CALLAHAN: Excuse me, dear. I'm sorry. Are you a Catholic?

EDMOND: Mrs Callahan.

MRS CALLAHAN: I'm only asking. A member of our congregation?

SHEILA: Not formally. No. *(Appealing to EDMOND)*

MRS CALLAHAN: Its just, we don't do that anymore.

(Beat. From SHEILA, *a question.* MRS CALLAHAN *touches the top of her head, referring to the lace* SHEILA *has clipped there.)*

MRS CALLAHAN: Not since the sixties, wouldn't you say, Father?

*(*EDMOND *gestures to* SHEILA, *at a loss.)*

SHEILA: Father doesn't look old enough to remember the sixties. But if it offends you, I'll pluck it off.

MRS CALLAHAN: Doesn't offend me, no. Brings me back, that's all.

*(*SHEILA *removes her head covering.)*

EDMOND: We're all right now, Mrs Callahan.

MRS CALLAHAN: I'll leave you, then.

*(*MRS CALLAHAN *leaves.* SHEILA *smiles at* EDMOND: *will they be able to share a joke about Mrs C? Immediately, she understands they won't, and loses her smile.* EDMOND *is not looking directly at her, as indeed he won't until she points it out.)*

EDMOND: Did we—actually—make an appointment?

SHEILA: No, actually. I guess I come from the old school. You have a problem, you go see your priest.

EDMOND: *(Beat)* That's a very old school, isn't it?

SHEILA: Well, I suppose I should confess. I've been dipping in—sitting in the back—on Sundays.
  Your sermons interest me. I wanted to come and talk to you. Also, there's something specific. May I sit down?

*(*EDMOND *nods, but gives no indication as to where she should sit.* SHEILA *takes a chair on the altar.* EDMOND *at first looks distressed by this. They are at a distance from one another.)*

SHEILA: *(Beat. Noticing his discomfort:)* Father, are you all right?

EDMOND: Yes. Perfectly fine. I was just wondering. Shall we go over to the rectory and I'll offer you— *(He pauses a moment, then comes up with what he clearly thinks is a good idea.)* —a cup of tea.

SHEILA: I'd just as soon not deal with your housekeeper again.

EDMOND: She's not—Mrs Callahan is not the housekeeper. We don't have live-in housekeepers anymore. *(A moment of embarrassment)* We're not allowed. Tea is actually the last thing I'd ever ask her to make. She does the books, the—bulletin. She volunteers. *(Beat)* I'd make the tea.

SHEILA: Thanks, but this is fine. *(Beat)* Except it makes you nervous.

EDMOND: *(Beat)* Mrs—

SHEILA: My name is Sheila Rosenthal. *(To his reaction:)* That's a Jewish name, Father, correct. I married a Jewish man. My maiden name is Mackey.

EDMOND: *(Pained to have to say it)* Mrs Rosenthal, congregants and pastors don't usually meet on the altar.

SHEILA: *(Perceiving the offence to be more serious than it is)* Oh. Oh my God. I'm sorry. *(She steps off the altar.)*

EDMOND: No. No. I mean, it's all right. Its my fault. I should have said something right away. Or nothing at all.

SHEILA: Tea would be fine. We can go to the rectory.

(She starts off, expecting him to follow. But he hesitates, looks back at the altar, uncertain about what he's just done, feeling foolish.)

SHEILA: Father.

(He follows, and the two of them immediately cross into the lighted space of the table and chairs stage left. There should be the sense that they have been talking before they enter; only in terms of stage time is this a continuous action.)

EDMOND: *(He immediately heads into an offstage room, while talking to her, so that all but the first sentence of the following is spoken offstage, while he is making tea.)* It's something I have to get over. It all has to do, I suppose, with your notion of the sacred.

   I know I need to move past this—dazzlement, really—with the altar. The whole church is sacred, the congregation, the *world*—there should be no limits on the sacred. It makes me feel incredibly young, and stupid.

SHEILA: Tell me. Would you have allowed us to sit there forever if I hadn't said?

EDMOND: I would have. But I wouldn't have heard a word you said. *(He returns, seems a bit nervous.)*

SHEILA: You haven't done this before, have you? Made tea?

EDMOND: No. I do take out.

SHEILA: Take out *tea*?

EDMOND: Pathetic, isn't it?

SHEILA: Father, you've been here—?

EDMOND: Six—no, five months.

SHEILA: No visits from lonely widows, in all that time?

EDMOND: *(Deciding to ask the question)* Is there something off-putting about me?

SHEILA: On the contrary.

EDMOND: People have not come forward, generally. I live for the occasional invitation to dinner.
   But I don't get any. Mrs Callahan does not cook for

me, and I wouldn't know where to begin. I am eating
take-out every night.

(A confession of some seriousness to him. She's amused by it.)

EDMOND: I thought people would come, that's all.

SHEILA: It's an island. It will take awhile before you're
accepted here.

EDMOND: I'm— *(Sudden realization, as he listens to
something offstage: the sound of the teakettle's whistle
slowly becoming louder)* Is that it? That's it, yes?

SHEILA: Let it get a little louder. It'll keep, Father.
You were saying—?

EDMOND: Sorry. I'm sorry. Is what I wanted to say.
Because you came, clearly, not to hear about me—

SHEILA: No. Let me be a test case for you, Father. The
first parishioner to come to you with a real concern.

(The whistle of the teapot is now full out, and he exits.)

EDMOND: Coming right up!

(After a few moments, EDMOND *comes back on with two
cups of tea.* SHEILA *stares at them. Beat.)*

SHEILA: And do you take milk, Father? Sugar?

EDMOND: *(Dashing off)* Of course. I'm sorry. I'll just be
a minute.

*(*EDMOND *comes back with milk and sugar on a makeshift
tray. Also, a bag of cookies.* SHEILA *will not touch her tea,
but* EDMOND *prepares his, and seems to have forgotten*
SHEILA *has come for any reason but for him to prepare tea.)*

EDMOND: There are cookies, I remembered. *(He takes
a cookie out, dips it into his tea, pleased with himself,
not offering her any.)*

SHEILA: Father, I've noticed you won't look directly
at me. Why is that?

(He still does not look at her, but doesn't answer either. It's as if a man unused to being aware of himself suddenly becomes aware of himself. He sits back, brushes cookie crumbs off his chest, waits for the conversational topic to change.)

SHEILA: Priestly secret. I won't pry.

EDMOND: *(Aware of not looking at her now, but painfully so)* The problem.

SHEILA: Hmm?

EDMOND: The specific concern you spoke of.

SHEILA: Oh. *My* problem. *(Beat)* I have a son, Father. He's eleven years old. He's never received communion.

(Beat)

EDMOND: *(Relief)* That's very simple.

SHEILA: *(Correcting him, firm but friendly)* No. It's not. When I married, I had no particular religion, lapsed something, like the rest of the world, Catholic in my case. My husband thought he might be the one more likely to return to the fold in time, so we tilted toward Judaism when our son was born.

EDMOND: And now you've changed your mind. It's simple enough.

SHEILA: *(Correcting him in the same firm but friendly manner)* No. It's not. My husband left us. He lives in Boston now. The only shred of Judaism left in our house is my son's lack of a foreskin. *(She smiles, acknowledges her very small joke.)* He's in a wheelchair, Father *(She takes a cookie. It breaks in her hand as she tries to eat it. She has to catch it as she goes on.)* He was born with a disease you've never heard of. At the time, only six children in the world were thought to have it. He can't see. He is fed through a tube in his stomach because of a problem with reflux that can always threaten to suffocate him.

(Beat. EDMOND *is looking at her now, against his own will. She catches him at it; he turns away.)*

SHEILA: There was a moment when Riley was three, when it became clear he might well survive for a number of years. It was suggested to me that he be institutionalized. "Placed" is actually the word they use. *(Beat)* There I was, with a three year old boy and images of myself pushing him in a wheelchair for the rest of his life. My husband had left social work to come to this island and become a painter. Me, I'm a nurse. We had certain dreams, Father. It would have been the logical thing to let him go. *(Beat)* You'll think this is odd. A "voice" appeared in my head. "Keep him," it said. Utterly clear. "Keep him." And then it disappeared. *(Beat)* I have fought the good fight for eight years. Now one of the things it occurs to me I could do is try and involve Riley more in my life. I go to church now, I've come back. I'm not sure what I believe, but I go. *(Checking with him)* I am waiting for that voice to appear again, I suppose, that moment of unambiguous clarity. So, perhaps—I thought—he could come with me. And when I walk down the aisle to receive communion— *(Again. Checking with him)* —well, maybe he could come with me there too. It could be I'm fooling myself, but there's my thinking.

(Silence)

EDMOND: *(At a loss for words, but having to come up with some)* The disease is called—?

SHEILA: Not that it matters, but it's called Canavan's disease. Technically, it's referred to as a leukodystrophy. Isn't this fascinating? He has spastic quadraparesis, chronic lung disease, a seizure disorder—shall I go on?

*(*MRS CALLAHAN *enters.)*

MRS CALLAHAN: Father, I just need you to check the bulletin before it's sent off to the printers.

EDMOND: Mrs Callahan, can't it wait? We're in the middle of something.

MRS CALLAHAN: Well, yes, it can wait. Yes, of course, but it's Thursday. We send it to the printers on Thursday so you can pick it up on Saturday. How did he do with the tea?

SHEILA: Well.

MRS CALLAHAN: Good. You haven't touched yours.

SHEILA: I don't drink tea. I was giving him practice.

(MRS CALLAHAN *takes them both in, sees that she's going to lose.*)

MRS CALLAHAN: Well, I'll come back. But it can't wait much longer, Father. It needs to go out today. *(She exits.)*

(Upon her exit, SHEILA *starts to laugh at* MRS CALLAHAN's *behavior.* EDMOND *silences her by not joining in.)*

EDMOND: The rule—it's a soft rule, I suppose—is that in order for a child to receive communion, he has to know what the host is. He has to be able to recognize it as the body and blood of Our Lord. Otherwise, it would be meaningless.

SHEILA: I'm not at all sure what Riley does and does not recognize, Father. But I don't imagine that "body and blood of Our Lord" is a concept Riley would be able to grasp. *(Beat. Uncomfortable)* So you're saying no.

EDMOND: *(A little helpless)* I could meet with him.

SHEILA: *(Acknowledging that; pleased, but trying to hide it.)* That would be—

EDMOND: We have a class of students. Six and seven year olds mostly. It meets on Sundays after Mass.

SHEILA: *(Slight smile)* I don't think Riley would get a lot out of meeting with your other students, Father. It might be easier if you came to him.

EDMOND: To your house.

SHEILA: Yes.

EDMOND: Of course.

SHEILA: *(She writes something down on a slip of paper.)* Here is my number. *(Reacting to his air of uncertainty)* If you don't mind my saying, you seem a bit nervous about this, Father.

EDMOND: *(Attempting to compensate for what she's picked up in him)* No, not at all. There's no neutral space at all, then?

SHEILA: Neutral space? There's the diner. If you want to see what it's like for me to feed my son through his G-tube while the other diners gawk, and sometimes complain, that would be fine. If you want to put me in yet another excruciatingly uncomfortable situation—

EDMOND: No. I apologize. Of course I'll come to your house. *(He reaches for the slip containing her number. She hands it to him.)*

SHEILA: *(Humble)* Thank you.

EDMOND: Would Wednesday afternoon be good?

SHEILA: We'll be home after one. We usually are. Any day. *(As she's about to exit:)*

EDMOND: That voice that appeared to you eight years ago, do you think of it as Our Lord's?

SHEILA: I did. I sometimes still do. But then we put the words "Our Lord" on so many things, don't we? We burn our hands, we cry out to him. We nearly get into a car accident, its "Jesus!" "God!" He's all-purpose, isn't he? We'll see you on Wednesday then, Father.

(She exits. After a moment, EDMOND *returns to the altar, looks around, bemused, uncertain about the encounter. He kneels to pray.)*

(The image on the screen above him fades from the cross to the mast of the ferry. A blood red sunset illuminates the stage as we segue to:)

Scene Four

(The ferry)

(A half-hour has passed since Scene One. DON *stands at the guardrail, intent on reading his guidebook.* BOB *remains in his seat. The red of the sunset plays against* DON's *face.)*

BOB: It will be empty, Donald. *(Beat)* The church.

*(*DON *looks confused.* BOB *points toward the island where they're headed.)*

DON: Yes. So it will. Abandoned.

BOB: Do you have another man to send there?

DON: At the moment, with the decline in vocations, you know very well I don't. Damn well better find one though, hmm?

BOB: Of course it could not be asked, not under the new dispensation, that I be assigned there.

But given the vague nature of the accusation against me, and the fact that nothing was ever fully established, I did wonder if perhaps as an interim—a stopgap—

DON: Oh, cut it out with the humility. It doesn't suit you. What are these monks doing to you? Let's see a little of the old arrogance. "Stopgap". You're a good priest, you've done your penance. If I want to assign you to this church, I can do it.

BOB: I hardly think so. If the papers were to pick it up—

DON: Yes, the papers. The damn papers. We constantly have to worry about the busybodies on *The Boston Globe*. Not enough child murders in Boston. Not enough corruption in city government. No, pick on the priests. Why I'm traipsing up there in the first place. To see if there's a scandal some cub reporter on *The Globe* can make his bones by reporting. I'd like to shove it in their faces. I'd like to appoint someone like you. A "spurious" charge, you say?

BOB: Yes.

DON: And only the one?

BOB: Only the one.

DON: Only one thing I need to know. Are you safe around young boys, Robert? *(Beat)* Are you?

BOB: Yes.

DON: Good enough for me.

(Beat. BOB's hopeful reaction is a silent one.)

DON: Hate it so much, do you? This new monk's life of yours?

BOB: *(Released, off his guard)* I am wasted there, that's all. I thought there would be more to do. Its quite a bleak life, really. Full of obedience. No room for the ego, I'm afraid. *(Opening up even more)* Then, too, they are a strange group of men. Not unlikable, really. But I find we have very little in common.

DON: Not even Our Lord, Robert? Curious, that.

BOB: *(Beat. Aware he's been caught)* Well, of course, Him.

DON: You've always struck me as a priest who'd have been a lot happier if the whole God part of the priesthood could somehow be left aside. A little distasteful, this God business, isn't it?

BOB: You underestimate me.

DON: Do I? Think how nice, a society of men, taken care
of, highly respected— *(Stops a moment)* —well, *formerly*
highly respected. A sinecure for life, time to read, all
the food and wine you want. And who really needs
Our Lord, after all? Moral behavior is enough, isn't it?
    To get up and say a few good things on Sunday.
Hardly need the Gospels to say "Be nice to each other",
do we?

BOB: You've always thought I was a kind of
ecclesiastical party boy, haven't you?

DON: Oh, I don't know.

BOB: In seminary, I was the kind of priest you hated.

DON: Hate's too strong. I thought you might well
destroy the Church, but hate's too strong.

BOB: We haven't quite destroyed the Church.

DON: No, but the party's over, isn't it? They're making
their grab. The people. The "laity".
    We've made a botch of it, that's their view. You've
made it so they feel justified in becoming watchdogs
over us. Trust is gone.

BOB: I hardly think it can all be blamed on the
homosexual clergy.

DON: Why not? You all thought you'd never be found
out? We're in glass houses. This boy—this priest on
this island—did he think no one would know what was
going on? What was he thinking?

*(As BOB speaks, RILEY is wheeled on by a man we haven't
yet met. RILEY is seated in his wheelchair, which is tilted
backward slightly to accommodate his most comfortable
position. He has a large head; his limbs are useless to him.
A tube goes into his throat; another connects to his stomach.
His head lolls; he clutches an ancient teddy bear. He looks
younger than his eleven years. While RILEY, and the next*

*scene, are being set up, the priests remain on stage,
finishing their scene.)*

BOB: He wondered who we were.

DON: We?

BOB: Yes. Priests.

*(On the screen, ferry mast fades to the image of a house,
and not a very good one. We are in:)*

Scene Five

(SHEILA's house)

*(As the lights open up to reveal the entirety of the scene
[which should take place within the small kitchen space
previously used for the rectory], we meet GARY, RILEY's
nurse, the man who wheeled RILEY on. GARY is large,
boisterous, wears his hair in a long ponytail. SHEILA is
offstage, cooking. It is Christmas time; small indicators
should reveal this.)*

*(GARY is using a nasal syringe to clean out RILEY's nose,
slowly and carefully. Golden oldies music is playing, and
GARY is singing along, talking to RILEY. There's a sense
of ongoing life here—routine—as EDMOND walks on with
his catechism.)*

GARY: Evening, Father.

EDMOND: Sheila asked if you could turn down the
music.

GARY: Is it bothering her? Go ahead, turn it down.
Its crap, but Riley likes it. Go ahead.

*(As EDMOND turns it down, GARY shouts to the offstage
SHEILA:)*

GARY: The music's bothering you, is it, Sheila?

SHEILA: *(Off)* Yes!

GARY: *(Still shouting off:)* What are we making in there? I can smell it. Something good. *(He notices* EDMOND's *catechism but doesn't comment.)*

EDMOND: *(Holds it up, slightly embarrassed)* What is it you're doing?

GARY: His nose. He can't blow it so it gets plugged up. Like to try it?

EDMOND: *(Assuming he's joking)* No.

GARY: So how's it going, this plan for communion?

(RILEY *has gotten fussy and resistant)*

GARY: Uh uh, Riley. Hmm?

EDMOND: Umm. Well.

GARY: *(Off, to* SHEILA:*)* Chicken livers! That's what it is, isn't it?

SHEILA: *(Off)* You've got it.

GARY: *(Squeezes some of the collected snot onto a paper towel)* Disgusting, isn't it? So go ahead, don't let me stop you with your lesson. Go right ahead.

EDMOND: She thought maybe you could help.

GARY: Help? How's that?

EDMOND: What do you think he understands?

GARY: *(Responding to the radio, which has begun to play* Shake Your Booty:*)* Oh, here's one you like, Riley. *(To* EDMOND, *as he turns the radio up:)* Sorry. One of his favorites. *(Off, to* SHEILA:*)* I'm turning it up. Hope it doesn't offend your sensibilities.

(RILEY *smiles to hear the song.* EDMOND *notices, intrigued, and* GARY *dances enthusiastically to the song, as if for* RILEY's *benefit.)*

GARY: This is something he definitely understands, Father. K C and The Sunshine Band's Letter to the Phillipians. *(He finishes with* RILEY's *nose.)* There. His nose is as clean as its going to get. He's all yours, Father.

*(*EDMOND *comes hear to* RILEY. *An awkwardness on his part.* GARY *steps back, turns down the music.)*

EDMOND: Hello, Riley. Its Father Ed.

*(*RILEY *smiles.)*

EDMOND: I still can't understand why he smiles.

GARY: No reason. He likes your voice. Go on.

EDMOND: Riley, I'd like to talk to you about— *(He is having a bit of difficulty.)*

GARY: God, I think is what you want to say.

EDMOND: Thank you.

GARY: Go ahead. Tell him.

EDMOND: *(Smiles, understanding a little of the absurdity)* It actually seems pretty silly.

GARY: Don't underestimate him. Nobody really knows how much Riley understands or doesn't understand. For all we know he could be taking in everything.

EDMOND: *(With forced confidence)* I'm here to talk about God, Riley.

*(*RILEY *smiles.)*

GARY: You see? He's familiar with God. From *God Only Knows* by the Beach Boys. *(Encouraging)* Go on. Talk to him like you'd talk to any child.

EDMOND: God made us— *(Turning back to* GARY, *as if he feels he has to explain his choices)* —what I say in my catechism class—God made us, first of all, in His image.

(GARY *is looking at* RILEY, *commenting to himself on the
"His image" reference: this is what God looks like? But
though he's respectful of* EDMOND *and says nothing,*
EDMOND *picks up on his attitude.)*

EDMOND: I don't mean to be rude. I think it would be
easier talking to him if you weren't here.

GARY: Father, a suggestion. Riley listens to the radio all
the time. Try some pop culture references.

EDMOND: I'm not sure I know any.

GARY: That isn't true. Sheila tells me you use—that
show, that Bill Bixby show—all the time. The Hulk,
is it? The Incredible Hulk.

EDMOND: I used it once.

GARY: No, no. She said it was fantastic.

EDMOND: I came out of the seminary understanding
nothing of what my parishioners would have seen,
would know. We had no television. But I would visit
my father—he's retired, the television was always
on—and one day I happened to catch that show.

GARY: *Nobody* remembers that show. Father, this is
hilarious. You thought you'd really *connect* with your
parishioners with that one. Oh yes, the Hulk, they'd
all say. I bet you don't even know they made it into a
movie.

EDMOND: They laughed.

GARY: Of course they did.

(SHEILA *enters.)*

SHEILA: I thought I'd see how you boys are doing.

GARY: Oh, we're getting along great. Discussing The
Hulk.

SHEILA: Don't tease him.

GARY: I'm not teasing. What are you cooking, by the way

SHEILA: Crostini.

GARY: *(Snaps his fingers, getting it.)* The chicken livers, of course.

SHEILA: *(Picking up on a certain tension coming from him.)* They'll be done soon. *(To* EDMOND:*)* Are you hungry?

EDMOND: Yes.

GARY: Not asking me?

SHEILA: This is a special dinner I'm making for Father Edmond, Gary. And I was hoping you could get Riley to bed early.

GARY: Ah. *(Clearly disappointed, but letting her off the hook)* Its fine, its fine, I don't have to be invited. Yes, I'll get him into bed early so that you two can have your—

SHEILA: *(There's an awkwardness now.)* Well, it'll be done soon. I want to give Riley some, too. Before you put him down.

GARY: I don't think so, not so close to his bedtime.

SHEILA: Just a taste. *(She exits.)*

GARY: Crostini. She doesn't cook crostini for me, I'll tell you that. *(Beat. Considering* EDMOND's *thickness:)* Doesn't it bother you even a bit?

EDMOND: What?

GARY: Nothing.

EDMOND: What should bother me?

GARY: Well. People are talking, Father. The car parked here til late at night. The divorcee with— *(He covers his mouth)* —did I say "a past"?

EDMOND: *(Almost laughing at the absurdity of it)* There's nothing. She asked me to come and prepare her son for a sacrament. What are you saying?

GARY: *(On the last of this exchange, he's gotten down and begun releasing the stays on* RILEY's *wheelchair.)* Listen. Would you like to try this? Freeing him up? Pushing him? Ever done this kind of work?

(Beat. EDMOND *has never considered this. Uncertainly,* EDMOND *gets up and takes over for* GARY, *releasing the stays. When the wheelchair is free, he pushes it, with some difficulty.)*

GARY: Sing to him, Father.

EDMOND: I don't know any of those songs.

GARY: Oh, surely before you went into the seminary you listened to the radio. High school?
    Never out on a date with a girl? Friday night. Never? What are you, twenty-nine, thirty?

EDMOND: I'm thirty-one.

GARY: So—mid eighties, you're a kid. Come on. Golden age. Sting. Howard Jones. Husker Du.
    Names mean anything to you? Hall and Oates?

EDMOND: Some of them, yes, actually.

GARY: Oh, give us a chorus of "One on One". *(Beat. Making something serious of the joke:)* Its all he needs, really.

*(*EDMOND *looks at* GARY *and laughs, uncomfortably.)*

GARY: What's so funny, Father?

EDMOND: The thought of me, I guess, singing "One on One".

GARY: *(After considering* EDMOND *for a long time, he points to a machine on stage.)* Do you know what this is, Father? Its an updraft machine. It administers medicine to open up the bronchial tubes, which get clogged when Riley wheezes, which he does when he regurgitates his phlegm—there's no controlling this boy, there's just a series of catastrophes to be averted.

EDMOND: *(Touching the machine)* Is he in danger?

GARY: Most of the time, yes. Terrible danger. But he goes on somehow, day after day, year after year. And now she wants him to—perceive it all. To know God. A boy who can't swallow, he's supposed to be thinking about God.

EDMOND: If someone could get through to him, I imagine it might be a comfort. To know something's waiting for him.

GARY: To know someone's waiting to wipe his bottom I would think might be a larger concern.
 Or get the snot out. I would think—

(Knowing his arguments are unanswerable, he allows EDMOND *to hang a moment before releasing him.)*

GARY: But perhaps I'm wrong, huh, Father? Well. Enough. *(Calling off:)* Sheila, I'm putting him down!

SHEILA: *(Off)* One minute. One. I'm coming. *(She enters with crostini, breaking it up in a bowl.)*

GARY: Its too close to his bedtime.

SHEILA: Just one. *(She pours the mixture into a syringe, then feeds it to* RILEY *through his stomach tube.)* Good, Riley? Is it good?

GARY: He's not smiling.

SHEILA: Goodnight, Riley. *(She kisses him, picks up his stuffed animal.)* Goodnight, Bunkie. *(Something just the slightest bit forced in these actions. We shouldn't know this for sure, but we should pick up a hint of the forced.)*

GARY: You want to say good night, Father?

EDMOND: Goodnight, Riley.

(GARY *exits, with* RILEY.)

SHEILA: *(Eager to keep the evening moving, offers* EDMOND *a crostini.)* They look a little dry to me. Taste one.

EDMOND: *(Eating)* Good.

SHEILA: How's your cooking coming along? *(She begins lighting candles around the room.)*

EDMOND: I cooked a chicken. That book you gave me—very helpful. It was pink, actually, inside.

SHEILA: Timing.

EDMOND: The little thermometer popped out.

SHEILA: *Never* trust those.

EDMOND: I'm learning about vegetables.

(SHEILA *has placed the candles around the room, so that the room has begun to look festive.)*

EDMOND: I can't stay late. I shouldn't.

SHEILA: Which is it—can't or shouldn't?

EDMOND: I'm not making much progress.

SHEILA: Riley likes having you here. He likes having a visitor.

EDMOND: That's all I am, though. I'm not teaching him anything. I mean—it seems pretty evident.

(SHEILA *shies away from responding, goes on arranging candles.)*

SHEILA: Does it look like Christmas yet?

EDMOND: I did some research. There's a place for boys like Riley, to prepare for the sacraments.
    It's not even very far from here. A few hundred miles. I'd be glad to take him. A place called Jericho. They have techniques for reaching boys like him, insofar as

they can be reached. It's not an institution. I know how you feel about institutions. He would go for a few days at a time.

SHEILA: Aren't we having a nice time? Why are you bringing up this Jericho place?

EDMOND: I sometimes think your inviting me here—forgive me—this is not about Riley at all.

SHEILA: *(Beat. Taking in his very surprising inference.)* Have I laid a trap for you, Father? Am I the femme fatale? Do I want to seduce you? Is that your fear, Father?

EDMOND: No.

SHEILA: Fed by—what? *The Thorn Birds*? Was your father watching that one afternoon when you dropped by, after seminary?

EDMOND: Stop this, please.

SHEILA: We're an island community. We're very small. There are very few people who can string eight words together in a comprehensible manner or who can stay sober on a Friday night in winter. Congratulations, you won the lottery.

EDMOND: How important is this issue of Riley receiving communion to you right now? Because I can tell you, in good conscience, that it's not working. *(Letting go of his formal manner with her)* Sheila, you see what's going on.

SHEILA: We're not friends, then?

(Beat. EDMOND simply looks at her, questioning.)

SHEILA: Friends. Simple. Friends. We're not friends?

(EDMOND still won't answer.)

SHEILA: I've invited you to dinner. I've been teaching you how to cook. When I met you, you were the take-out king of the island. Now you're not. You used to wish for invitations. *(Finally showing her anger)* Edmond, if you don't mind my saying it, the last thing I expected of you was a cheesy mind.

EDMOND: I'm sorry.

SHEILA: Good. You should be.

EDMOND: Gary told me people were talking.

SHEILA: About *us*? Oh, fuck him. Fuck you, Gary. Jealousy, pure and simple. *(To* EDMOND'*s unspoken question:)* Yes, once. Oh, horrible. Don't make me think about it. There are levels of desperation, you can't imagine. *(Beat)* Maybe you should go.

EDMOND: *(Eats a crostini, apologetically)* Delicious.

SHEILA: I don't feel any level of comfort at this moment. I had planned a nice meal.

EDMOND: Sheila, I apologize. Once upon a time, a priest was free—to do this. Once upon a time no one would think... But so much has happened. In a small community, I'm afraid people talk.

SHEILA: Let them.

EDMOND: No. I have superiors. I have something to uphold. If the wrong word were to get back to them, I could be replaced here.

SHEILA: Then go. I'll feed Gary the chicken. Afterward we can maybe watch wrestling. What a swell night for me that would be. My mind is going to dangerous places, and you're afraid to *stay here* because of what people might say.

EDMOND: I will stay and eat the meal. But maybe I should start to come less.

SHEILA: As you wish. *(She goes into the built-in cupboards, finds a bottle of wine.)*

EDMOND: What "dangerous places"? *(Beat)* You said your mind is going to dangerous places.

SHEILA: I thought I would tell you about that, but not tonight. I didn't want to use it as a way of holding you here.

(Beat. EDMOND *waits, as she begins to uncork the wine.)*

SHEILA: I'd rather wait to talk about it, if you don't mind, until Gary leaves.

EDMOND: I have to leave when Gary leaves.

SHEILA: Fine, then. *(Beat. As she speaks, she continues the process of uncorking the wine.)* That voice we talked about—that voice of maybe God, from eight years ago? It's come back. Only it's telling me something very different now. *(She pauses briefly. When the wine is uncorked, wherever she is in the following speech, she pours herself a glass.)* The ferry ride. Weekly. To see Riley's neurologist on the mainland. Father, when you spend a lot of time with a child, even a healthy child, there's a certain degree of boredom to be overcome. You're moving according to someone else's clock. With Riley, I am always moving more slowly. So, when there's a *reason* to rush, we tend to get there early.

*(*EDMOND *tilts his head, not sure where this is leading.)*

SHEILA: We're always first in line for the ferry, is what I'm saying. *(Beat)* We sit in the car, waiting, and there is a rope in front of us, until the ferry approaches. Then, when the ferry is still three hundred feet or so out to sea, a man comes and unties the rope, And for a few minutes there is nothing between us and the ferry but the open sea. *(Beat)* To make a long story short, Father, what that voice is telling me now is: "Drive. Go ahead." The rope is lifted, the sea is before me, the ferry is two hundred feet away. For two years, I've been coming to church, waiting to hear God's voice again, this is what

has come instead. "Go. Drive. Why wait? The two
of you, into the sea." I grit my teeth, I bite my wrist
sometimes to make this fantasy, this *voice*, go away.
(She displays to him, casually, the marks on her wrist.)

EDMOND: You never would.

SHEILA: I wonder.

EDMOND: No. you never would.

SHEILA: The chicken should be ready.

*(She goes off. EDMOND sits at the table she has set. He puts
his head in his hands and says a prayer. SHEILA comes back
on with the chicken on a tray. She observes him praying,
touched. He looks up.)*

SHEILA: Were you praying for me?

EDMOND: Yes. *(She places the chicken before him,
begins dishing it out.).*

SHEILA: The secret to chicken is to take it out of the oven
and let it continue to cook. The secret to vegetables is
don't take a phone call when you've got them on the
stove.

*(She pours him some wine, or attempts to. He covers his wine
glass, shakes his head.)*

EDMOND: You never would.

(She pours herself wine, starts to eat.)

SHEILA: Merry Christmas, Father Ed.

*(He looks at her, not knowing what to think. Certainly not
hungry.)*

SHEILA: You're not eating.

EDMOND: You can't—say something like that to
someone, and expect them to carry on as if this were
a normal night.

SHEILA: Why not? It's normal to me. The routines of my week. *(As if she's checking things off a list:)* Take him to the neurologist. Fight the desire to kill us both. I mean, I sit here and I *hope* I don't do it. I want to go on living among the sane and the dutiful. But I know that when Tuesday comes, and we are in line for that ferry, that voice will come back.

EDMOND: There are—I mean, some obvious things you can do, aren't there? Leave a little later. Don't be first in line. Is there family, Sheila—do you have family on the mainland?

(She looks at him, doesn't answer.)

EDMOND: He could still be institutionalized—placed.

SHEILA: Could he? Yes. Yes, he could. *(Beat. She puts down her fork.)* I don't think you get me at all, do you?

EDMOND: No. Sometimes—no.

SHEILA: When I chose to keep him at home, Father—. *(She pauses, something difficult in this.)* When I heard that voice eight years ago, it didn't come as a sporting challenge. It didn't come as a wager I could lose. I allowed it to change me, Father. You don't spend eleven years living day in, day out with a child and then act as though you can say, okay, enough, this is getting too damned hard. I am connected to him. I couldn't let him go now. *(Beat)* Could you do that? Live without your relationship to your God?

EDMOND: If the alternative was suicide, I would consider—

SHEILA: *(Disbelieving)* Would you?

EDMOND: And the death of a child, yes.

SHEILA: Really? Your calling to God is so revocable? Squeeze out of it if it gets too hard? What a nice calling to have!

EDMOND: If something leads to suicide, Sheila, it's not a calling.

SHEILA: No? But what if god's crafty, Father? What if he wants to test us? Take us to the limit. Jesus in the desert, fasting. Wasn't that the moment when the devil came in? What if this is—excuse me—the devil talking to me?

EDMOND: (*A moment of consideration. Being careful with her, but vaguely superior.*) We don't really talk about the devil anymore.

SHEILA: Oh, we don't, do we? Why not?

EDMOND: He was once a convenient symbol, but we now prefer to speak in terms of an absence.

SHEILA: Well, that's fine for you, Father, but its more convenient for me to talk in terms of a little red guy with a pitchfork and a tail. He's sitting beside me in the car, saying: What do you need this for? Go ahead. (*Beat*) Because maybe—well, maybe this is one of God's odd ways—maybe we are near the end. Sometimes I get a strange inkling of that. Maybe there is only a little bit longer to go.
     And it stands to reason—to me—that that would be the moment when the pressure might build, and explode.

EDMOND: (*Beat. Careful*) I think you're right to see it as a temptation. But God does not offer us temptations we're not strong enough to resist.

SHEILA: Bullshit. Bull*shit*. Ever see Caravaggio's painting of Abraham sacrificing Isaac?

(*Beat.* EDMOND's *reaction is a kind of disbelief.*)

SHEILA: Yes, I am smart enough to know paintings, Father. (*She throws down her napkin.*) So there's your old world patriarch Abraham. And in every classic Bible image he's got the long beard, the soulful eyes lifted to heaven: why, God, why do you ask me to do this? But in Caravaggio, who maybe knew a thing or two about how things work down here on earth, there's Abraham holding the knife with a look on his face like he can't wait to do the deed.

And poor Isaac is screaming, and even the lamb in the corner is looking terrified, and the angel sent by God is wearing a look that says: uh oh. Uh oh.

Maybe God misjudges sometimes, Father. Being not quite human. He misjudges that desire we have to just be rid of it all. That impulse to say: *enough.* God must always be surprised. Uh oh. Too big of a burden on that one.

EDMOND: The fact is Abraham held back at the last moment.

SHEILA: *(Scorn) Fact.*

EDMOND: Not fact. All right. In the *story.* It's a story. It never happened, and it happened. It never happened and it's true.

SHEILA: An angel came, yes. *(Beat)* At the last moment. Am I correct? Stayed Abraham's hand. At the last moment. An angel. How God works. He sends angels. *(Beat)* Helpmates. Friends.

(They look at each other a moment. GARY enters.)

GARY: He's down.

SHEILA: Really down, or "down"?

GARY: Really down, I think. *(Beat)* So I'll go.

SHEILA: *(Looks at her watch)* What if he wakes? He does that. You've still got another hour. Why don't you stay with him?

GARY: *(Stung a little bit)* "With him"? Look, would it kill you to share some of this— *(Recognizes the dish SHEILA has cooked)* Chicken Marbella.

SHEILA: You've got it.

GARY: You do the bay leaves?

(SHEILA *holds one up.*)

GARY: You telling me there's not enough for three? I've gotta go eat at the bar?

(SHEILA *looks at* EDMOND, *not to see if he'll agree, but to be sure he'll go along with her* not *agreeing.*)

SHEILA: I only made enough—. I thought Father might take the rest back to the rectory. *(Pronounced)* When he leaves. You son of a bitch.

GARY: What?

SHEILA: People are not talking about us.

GARY: Ah. All right. *(Beat. Stops on his way out.)* By the way. Riley asked me a question in there: the transubstantiation of the host, how exactly does that work? He wants to know. *(Exiting)* Tomorrow then, hmm? *(He exits.)*

EDMOND: *(Beat)* It occurs to me sometimes that the world is so much more lonely than I am. Me, who lives in a rectory, by himself. God is in that car with you. He is there. You only have to feel him. He is there.

SHEILA: Is he? What if he misplaced me, Father? So many of us to worry about, one or two of us must fall through the cracks. One or two of might need some assistance.

(*There is a sound, from* RILEY, *interrupting her.*)

SHEILA: Oh God, I knew he shouldn't have left. *(She starts to go.)*

EDMOND: What does he need?

SHEILA: *(Beat)* I don't know. Sometimes just to be gentled.

EDMOND: I could try that.

(She looks at him.)

SHEILA: Go ahead.

(He goes off. She waits, and as she does, DON and BOB come on, stand near the rope, as the ferry approaches the dock. They are facing the island, staring at it as it draws near. The two scenes should now play simultaneously, SHEILA waiting while DON and BOB have their dialogue.)

DON: That's it, then. The island. Did we hear him right?

BOB: I think so. Yes.

DON: So small, isn't it? I expected something larger. *(Beat)* No time for anything tonight, I don't suppose.

BOB: No.

DON: Tomorrow we'll ask questions. Questions.

BOB: That is, if anyone will speak to us.

DON: Oh, they will. You can be sure of that. A bishop's robes still mean something. We'll have a look around. And I suppose we should visit the graves. *(Beat)* Not a large cemetery, I wouldn't assume.

BOB: No, I don't imagine it would be.

(EDMOND comes on, holding RILEY, singing softly to him. SHEILA watches him. EDMOND looks at her, a little helpless now, goes on singing.)

EDMOND: Is this all right?

SHEILA: Yes. That's fine.

EDMOND: His tubes are—?

SHEILA: Fine. You're doing fine.

DON: And we'll discover, God willing, what it was our young friend was so convinced God was calling him to do.

(As the ferry makes the sound of docking, the FERRYMAN *comes between* DON *and* BOB. *They part for him. The* FERRYMAN *stands waiting for the rope to be thrown him.* EDMOND *continues rocking* RILEY, *singing to him, the old Hall and Oates song* One on One, *while questioning* SHEILA *with his eyes, making sure what he is doing is alright.* SHEILA *watches, approving, drinking her wine.)*

(Lights fade)

END OF ACT ONE

ACT TWO

Scene One

(The ferry dock, several weeks after the events of ACT ONE, Scene Five.)

*(*SHEILA *and* RILEY *are seated on benches representing a car.* RILEY *is in the backseat, in his wheelchair.)*

(Immediate blast of sound: the golden oldie Sooner or Later [Love is Gonna Get Ya])

(They are waiting for the ferry. Onscreen: outline of the port.)

*(*SHEILA *is tense, looking straight out front.)*

SHEILA: *(She turns the music down.)* We are early. We tried to be late today, Riley, but we still got here early. *(A moment of simply staring ahead, blank-faced. Then her panic rises, and she has to get out of the car. She stands beside it, catching her breath.)* Do you miss the music? Should I just suffer through it, Riley? *(She turns to him.)* Why don't you tell me? Send me something.

(The FERRYMAN, *from* Scene One, *now the guardian of the rope, enters, stands to the side, lifts the rope guarding the dock, ready to remove it as the ferry approaches.)*

FERRYMAN: Ferry coming. Go on, get inside your car.

*(*SHEILA *looks at him.)*

SHEILA: Do I have to?

FERRYMAN: *(Looking at her, incredulous)* Yeah.

SHEILA: When it's here, I'll get in.

FERRYMAN: *(Beat)* Do you have a ticket?

SHEILA: *(As she reaches into her bag, takes her ticket out)* You only see me here every week.

FERRYMAN: Wait in the car, okay? The ferry's gonna be here any minute. If you're not gonna wait in the car, you have to get out of line.

(She looks at him, does. She sits in the car, staring out at the sea. FERRYMAN opens the rope, so there is nothing now between SHEILA and the water. She stares ahead, with great difficulty. After a long moment of forcing herself to do this— we should have the impression of her lashing herself to the mast—she looks in the back at RILEY. The sight of him comes as an odd kind of relief, a leveler. She stays on him as EDMOND rushes in, sits beside her.)

EDMOND: I'm sorry. I'm late.

(SHEILA looks at him, breathing more calmly now.)

EDMOND: The nursing home. A woman was holding my hand, and wouldn't let go. It was hard to leave. Just made it, looks like. *(He looks at his watch, turns to the back seat.)* Hey, Riley. How's Riley? *(Back to SHEILA:)* Were you okay?

SHEILA: Fine, yes.

EDMOND: You want me to drive?

SHEILA: No, I'm okay.

EDMOND: You mad cause I'm late?

SHEILA: No.

EDMOND: She wouldn't stop holding my hand. An old woman. Alice McGovern. *(He smiles, remembering. Then he punches in the music. The golden oldie* Brandy.*)* There you go, Riley. There's your music. *(He touches* RILEY. *To* RILEY:*)* Okay?

SHEILA: *(Watching him enjoying the music, a kind of wonder to her.)* You like this?

EDMOND: I've never heard it before.

(She goes on watching him, as he immerses himself in a culture new and therefore fresh to him, but tired and trying to her. EDMOND *checks on* RILEY *again, then stares ahead, as she does.)*

(Cross-fade to:)

Scene Two

(The Rectory)

(This is the same space where SHEILA *and* EDMOND *drank tea in* ACT ONE, *now slightly transformed. A computer is on the table, which now functions as a desk. The computer screen is lit at the top of the scene, as* MRS CALLAHAN *leads* DON *and* BOB *on.)*

(On the screen above the stage: an image of the church.)

MRS CALLAHAN: We're all computerized, of course.

DON: I'm impressed.

(BOB hangs back, allowing DON to dominate.)

MRS CALLAHAN: A project that has taken years, believe me. The list of parishioners goes back ten. You'll find a list over here in the right hand column of how much every family has contributed, going back—oh, five years now.

(DON has sat down before the console and begun pushing buttons. He turns to BOB:)

DON: You understand these?

BOB: A little.

DON: *(To* MRS CALLAHAN:*)* Where do I find the numbers?

MRS CALLAHAN: Scroll down.

DON: Hmm?

MRS CALLAHAN: I could do it for you.

DON: No, no. Which is the scroll button?

MRS CALLAHAN: Here.

DON: Broken down by islands, are they?

MRS CALLAHAN: No, not by islands. That list would be somewhere else.

DON: Is this it? The number? Four hundred and seventy-three?

MRS CALLAHAN: Active. Yes.

DON: Four hundred and seventy-three. And how many actually showed up?

MRS CALLAHAN: At the weekend masses, about a third of that. Usually.

DON: Some of them had to travel here, over distances, take the ferry.

MRS CALLAHAN: Oh yes.

DON: Well, thank you, Mrs—Callahan. Now we'd like to ask a different set of questions.

MRS CALLAHAN: Bishop, a group of us would be honored to have you to dinner. You and Father, of course.

(Beat. DON *considers her.)*

DON: That's very kind. But this is not a ceremonial visit.

MRS CALLAHAN: Of course, we understand. But we don't get a bishop often. It wouldn't be much, you understand, just a pot roast.

DON: Very kind. But Father Sullivan and I are going to fast while we're here.

(Beat. BOB *looks surprised.)*

DON: Yes. In honor of the dead. Something light, we'll have. Bread and soup.

MRS CALLAHAN: It's not so much the dinner, Bishop. It's that we'd like to talk.

(Beat. DON *gives her space.)*

MRS CALLAHAN: We'd like to have some input as to who's next here—who's to follow Father Leblanc.

*(*DON *takes this as a kind of effrontery, but sits on his response.)*

MRS CALLAHAN: There are special needs here, Bishop. The congregation has been thinning out. We thought an older man might bring them back. Someone safe. someone steady.
   It wouldn't take much.

DON: Yes, well, I'll certainly take that into account. *(To shift the topic:)* Mrs Callahan, I find it damp in here. Could you make us some tea?

MRS CALLAHAN: Tea? Of course. I'm not sure what the Father kept here. I believe I saw some earl grey.

DON: Earl grey. Oh, that sounds good. Father Sullivan?

BOB: Nothing, no.

MRS CALLAHAN: Do you take milk?

DON: I do. And sugar.

(Beat. She goes off.)

DON: An older man. They want to tell me who to send here. *(An outburst. He's had to hold a great deal in with* MRS CALLAHAN.*)* Are we becoming a church of old women, Father? Hmm? Are we here merely to succor

those for whom all the sweetness of life is gone? Stand
up in the pulpit and say, Worry not, dears. Heaven is
near. I'm sorry, we need this woman. I know that, but
I'll be damned if I'm going to eat their overcooked pot
roast tonight.

BOB: It might have been polite.

DON: I want some escape, dammit, from churchiness
while I'm here. There's a shore dinner I saw advertised
by the side of the road on the way here. Big poster, did
you notice? I believe it's called Hettie's Clam Shack.

BOB: And they serve a soup and bread special for
fasting priests.

DON: Fourteen ninety-five, the sign said. I deserve to
have a decent time while I'm here, do I not? Don't want
to listen to the yammering of the parishioners.

BOB: Its no sin for the laity to seek a voice in church
affairs.

DON: No. Indeed no. I can envision the day when
we'll have one of those squawkboxes outside of every
church, the kind they have at McDonald's. *(Mimics the
voice of a McDonald's waitress)* "What kind of church
would you like? Would that be large or small?" And
a priest? Would you like a priest with that as well?
Or can you do it all yourselves? "An older man".
Come on. Let's take a look.

BOB: The tea is coming.

DON: She'll bring it to us.

(Lights up on altar area, as DON *and* BOB *pass into it
without having exited the stage. The cross appears on
the screen above the altar as they look around.)*

DON: A little gem, isn't it?

(They are both looking at the ceiling.)

BOB: Needs paint.

DON: I don't think so. I like ruin. A church should reek a bit of death, don't you think?

BOB: I don't actually. I know you'll be shocked by that.

DON: *(Not really having heard what* BOB *has just said)* Ever seen—some monastery in Europe, I forget which one—wonderful painting on the wall, the Grim Reaper leaning over the monks' everyday activities, *greedily, hungrily,* and the words written on the painting, "Tonight, perhaps?" Love that.

BOB: Yes, embrace death, shall we? That's the way to bring the congregation back.

DON: I suppose you think you could do that? Make this old place a going concern. Are you their dream "older man"?

BOB: These are people needing to be gone out to. Father Leblanc was not socially gifted.

DON: Is that what we need to be now? Cruise directors of the spiritual life? Welcome to the Catholic Church, otherwise known as the Carnival Line to Golgotha. *(Beat)* Everyone thinks they can draw in the crowds by serving God-lite. Man I have over in Goshen— built up a huge congregation based on Saturday night musicales. Packs 'em in. *(With large innuendo:)* He sings, and his *friends* sing. Every Saturday night. The Gospel according to Jerry Herman. There's a church for you. Full pews. Healthy collections. But it's not *the* Church. And soon he'll be gone, that pastor, we're counting the days for him, and where will they be, those good people who learned to see no important distinction between God and *Mame*? *(Picks up the empty chalice from the altar, dusts it with his sleeve.)* Perhaps I should give all this up and come here myself. Take over this little parish.

BOB: And watch the numbers plummet.

DON: Watch yourself.

BOB: Donald, the reason you were promoted to Bishop is because you were considered too harsh for any congregation.

DON: *(Smiling)* Do you remember old Tom O'Brien? Before his retirement?

BOB: Before his gently forced retirement.

DON: Standing up before a congregation of working mothers. "When I was a boy, we used to come home from school, our mothers would be waiting. *With soup."* *(He laughs.)*

BOB: Yes, the "with soup" is what did it.

DON: Emptied out his parish. Oh, he was splendid.

BOB: Down to a congregation of old women at the end, as I recall, before they replaced him.

DON: Yes, but he had a point. Challenge them to think beyond the secular truths of their own time. But no, no, we flatter them. Thank you Alderman Kennedy for the gift of the flowers, and Alderman Kennedy in the fourth row beams. But we both know what Jesus would say to Alderman Kennedy. Empty those pockets. Come on, what else do you have to give? Empty yourself or you're doing *nothing. (To* BOB's *unspoken reaction:)* What? I suppose you want to go along with all this pressure to make us just like them? "Marry", shall we? Invite them up here to take over our jobs while we scamper off and attend to our "relationships"?

BOB: Well, why not? We've been pretending for nineteen centuries that we don't live inside our own bodies.

DON: I'll put you in this church, should I decide, because its empty and it needs someone, but not because I subscribe to the thinking that what you have done is a portent of some necessary change.

BOB: *(Beat. Taken aback for a moment)* We both know I have done nothing.

DON: *(A shade removed from apologetic)* Yes. *(Beat)* Yes. Forgive me. But I wonder. That boy who charged you. What happened to him while you were doing nothing? What did he suppose happened to him? Hmm?

BOB: I couldn't guess.

DON: Oh come on, Robert. Boys don't make up charges out of nothing.

BOB: Some do.

DON: Come. How am I to arrive at any judgment if you won't come clean with me.

BOB: There are reports you might read.

DON: Formal. They say nothing.

BOB: *(As frustrated as we will see him become)* I will not prostrate myself over a trumped-up charge. This is prostration enough, this monk-hood. I did not want to embarrass the Church, so I disappeared while this was being investigated. Now I want something back.

(MRS CALLAHAN enters, with tea, interrupting them.)

MRS CALLAHAN: Oh, there you are. I looked for you all over the rectory. Tea will be cold now.

DON: Not to worry. We just couldn't wait to see it.

(She hands it to him. He is excessively polite now.)

DON: Thank you.

MRS CALLAHAN: *(Uncomfortable, not sure she is invited to stay)* It needs paint, don't you think?

DON: So Father Sullivan believes.

MRS CALLAHAN: My children were baptized here.
There used to be a font. *(She points to a corner of the altar.)*

DON: Yes, and now the only font is on your computer,
isn't it? The old ecclesiastical language doesn't pass
away, Mrs Callahan. It transmutes into something more
practical. *(Catches himself; trying to be on his best behavior
with her.)* You were telling us. How many children do
you have?

MRS CALLAHAN: *(Cautious with him now, but facing
him down)* Four. Bishop. *(Beat)* Bridget. Kathleen. Jim.
Nancy.

DON: Three girls and a boy.

MRS CALLAHAN: That's right.

DON: Mrs Callahan, there's something very important
for us to know. We have a tragedy to deal with. What
does the Church have to answer for? Is there some
scandal we should be aware of? I'm speaking of Father
Leblanc's relations with this woman.

MRS CALLAHAN: *(Careful)* He would go to her house
and she would cook for him. Beyond that, I know
nothing.

DON: Have the papers been snooping around, Mrs
Callahan? Have they put things together? The deaths,
his disappearance?

MRS CALLAHAN: No, no they haven't. She was known
to be unsettled.

DON: Unsettled.

MRS CALLAHAN: Yes. Psychologically.

DON: And the coincidence of a man who used to eat at
her house disappearing?

MRS CALLAHAN: It was clearly ruled as—you know
what it was ruled as. Bishop, I'm unclear what you're

driving at. He was a misguided man, but he was an
honest man. An innocent, in my opinion.

DON: Really? An innocent. That's what they said about
Thomas Jefferson. Then the DNA comes along and we
find he was the Warren Beatty of the Enlightenment.

MRS CALLAHAN: He visited her. But there was nothing
like that in it. It was her problem. Her specific problem
with her little boy. He talked about it with me.
I think from the time he came here he was looking
for something to absorb him. I think he was
heartbroken when the event happened.

DON: Is that the story people are telling?

MRS CALLAHAN: There are always rumors, of course.

DON: What rumors?

MRS CALLAHAN: I don't want to dignify them.

DON: Dignify them, please.

MRS CALLAHAN: The usual. That he had—wronged her.
That this was the cause of what happened.

DON: And people are spreading these rumors.

MRS CALLAHAN: Unfortunately.

DON: Until someone on the mainland—the Castine *Post*,
the Lobsterville *Gazette*—sends an investigative
reporter over. And his story gets into the *Globe*. And
suddenly I'm getting a call from Rome.

MRS CALLAHAN: They are rumors, Bishop. They are
founded on nothing. Eventually any reporter would
have to come to me.

DON: To confirm or deny.

MRS CALLAHAN: Yes.

DON: Perhaps a pot roast—perhaps a pot roast would
not be such a bad thing, Mrs Callahan.

MRS CALLAHAN: The others will be pleased.

DON: *(Craftily seguing)* And tell us if you would, Mrs Callahan, one more thing. You know I don't have a lot of men to send here. Suppose, of necessity, I were to send you a priest around whom there is a kind of cloud.

(MRS CALLAHAN looks at him questioningly.)

DON: A priest informed on by an altar boy. But a vague, unprovable accusation. Never denied or proved either way.

MRS CALLAHAN: *(Beat)* You're not drinking your tea.

DON: You were right. Its cold. *(Beat)* Mrs Callahan.

MRS CALLAHAN: Is that all, Bishop?

DON: I am seeking your opinion.

MRS CALLAHAN: We wouldn't like it, Bishop. I can tell you that. I don't know, perhaps its none of our business. But given the shock of Father Leblanc's leaving, I don't think so. *(Beat)* Anything else, Bishop?

DON: No. That'll do. Thank you very much, Mrs Callahan. Perhaps—later.

(She exits.)

BOB: *(Sitting on his anger)* Why did you bring me if your mind is so made up?

DON: Who said its made up? I need that woman, Robert. At least for the moment, I need her. Though I think she has no true forgiveness in her. Do you believe her? About this young priest, I mean.

BOB: Knowing him as I do, yes.

DON: An innocent.

BOB: Yes.

DON: An innocent. Come, let's go and see the graves.

(He exits, and then, after a moment alone, so does BOB.*)*

(The church darkens, EDMOND *comes on, and we are in:)*

Scene Three

*(*EDMOND *crosses in front of the altar, makes the sign of the cross, lights a candle so that the primary light in the church now is candlelight.* EDMOND *is dressed in sweatclothes.)*

(At the same time, on the others side of the stage, RILEY *appears, in his wheelchair. The computer console has become a T V screen, shedding light on him. For the first part of the scene, it is extremely important to maintain the sense of two separate spaces, with the primary sources of light coming from the candle and the T V.)*

*(*EDMOND *kneels before the altar, but in side view so that we can see his face at least in profile. He attempts to pray. After a moment or two, we can see that he is having trouble. He looks up at the cross as if he's wondering for the first time what he's supposed to see there. Again, he attempts to lose himself in prayer. Can't. Some exclamation—a frustrated longing. He stares again at the cross, a great sorrow coming out of him. Then he stands up abruptly, blows out the candle and exits behind the altar, to reappear, holding a bowl of popcorn he's just popped, in* RILEY's *space—which is* SHEILA's *house—just as the lights fill out that space.)*

EDMOND: What do you want to see, Riley? You want to watch the animal channel? *(He checks on* RILEY *so he's comfortable. He fixes* RILEY's *hair, cleans his face. He stands, looking down at* RILEY *the way a man might stare at his own son. Some part of him resists this feeling. He seems about to offer* RILEY *some of the popcorn, then realizing the absurdity, holds it back, then puts it down. He gets down on his haunches, flips through channels on the T V. Lands on a rerun of* Growing Pains. *Becomes excited.)* Oh, this one. Remember this one, Riley?

(He sits down at RILEY's *side to watch the show. There are sounds from* RILEY. EDMOND *is alert to them. He checks* RILEY's *connections.)*

EDMOND: You all right?

*(*RILEY *puts his face forward, to be touched.* EDMOND *seems about to do it, but he's not sure: is it allowed? At a sound, he draws his hand away.)*

*(*SHEILA *comes in, with shopping bags.)*

SHEILA: Oh. He's still awake.

EDMOND: *(A certain guilt)* I kept him up.

(He nods toward the T V. SHEILA *goes to check what's on.)*

SHEILA: Are you aware that T V isn't *entirely* reruns?

EDMOND: I think I do know that.

SHEILA: *(Drops the bags, begins putting groceries away.)* Anyway, I'm grateful. I love an empty supermarket at night. No screaming babies. The lonely stockboys piling up cans. This sort of Edward Hopper meets *Dawson's Creek* landscape. I like your getup, by the way.

*(*EDMOND *looks down at himself, as if unaware of what he's wearing.)*

SHEILA: Frat boy chic.

(He shrugs, turns off the T V.)

SHEILA: Oh, don't— *("Because of me", is what she means.)*

EDMOND: No, I should get back, read my office—

SHEILA: *(Gentle mocking)* You should get back and be a priest is what you mean. *(Pulling back)* Sorry. What's an "office"?

EDMOND: Prayers. Daily prayers. Listen, want me to get him down?

SHEILA: That would be nice.

*(EDMOND wheels RILEY off. SHEILA continues putting
groceries away, remembers something. Calls off:)*

SHEILA: Edmond? He might need the chloral hydrate.
*(She checks her watch, goes back to finishing the groceries.
Then, when everything is put away, she turns on some
music. She pours herself some wine, flops down in a chair.
But there's something other than pure relaxation on her face.)*

*(After a minute, EDMOND comes on, carrying his sneakers.
SHEILA doesn't see him at first. He stands out of her sight,
studying her.)*

EDMOND: Down.

SHEILA: *(Slightly startled)* Hmm? Didn't need rocking?

EDMOND: No.

SHEILA: Wasn't fussy?

EDMOND: Uh uh.

SHEILA: He likes you.

*(Uncomfortable now, EDMOND's response is to begin putting
on his sneakers.)*

SHEILA: Edmond, what's the matter?

*(He looks up at her, but continues to put on and tie his
sneakers.)*

SHEILA: Can't I interest you in some wine?

EDMOND: No. Thank you.

SHEILA: *(She watches him.)* Edmond, you have no one
else to talk to, I know that. And it's very clear you need
to talk,

EDMOND: *(Deliberately downplaying it)* Its not such a big
thing. My prayer life is giving me trouble. *(Laughs,
as if to lighten it)* I bet that seems a very small thing.
A priest's prayer life.

SHEILA: If I understood prayer, I might be able to tell you whether it seems small. Why don't you tell me? Why don't you explain prayer to me?

EDMOND: *(Hesitates at first)* No, you can't really do that. Its not to be explained.

SHEILA: I think that's just priests' mumbo jumbo. You don't want the rest of us to have the power, so you keep it to yourself.

EDMOND: *(Rising to the challenge)* All right. When you are—when you go around all day, basically denying your needs, a tension starts up in the body. Things are held. They form a kind of ball, a nucleus that gets tight. And I think, I mean I believe, that for most people the place that gets released is in sex.

SHEILA: *(Beat)* That would be reasonable.

EDMOND: Except, for me—well, suppose that for someone that release was impossible.

SHEILA: I would imagine then a life of extreme frustration.

EDMOND: No, see, that's where you're wrong. That knot, that ball of tension, at the end of the day, or whenever, you kneel down and release it, you offer it to God, and something—floods in. This force. The empty space gets filled by this force.

SHEILA: It sounds wonderful. So why are you having trouble? *(Seeing his hesitation, coaxing:)* Edmond.

EDMOND: Prayer needs to be pure. You have to empty yourself. You have to—think about the cross. You can't be thinking about another person. I mean, you can pray for another person. But you have to do that within the context of the cross. *(Beat. He seems to know he's obfuscating. He seems to know, too, that* SHEILA *will not buy this.)* I kneel down, and I find myself thinking exclusively about Riley. *(Having said even that much loosens a rush of feeling in him.)* I kneel down, I say, alright then, he's in your head, pray, pray in the context of suffering, but the thought comes in: why not do something? I mean, Jesus didn't just die, he didn't just die on the cross, he—acted. He helped. I mean, isn't that the whole basis of his teaching? To give. To—well. Sometimes I really don't see the point of leaving this house.

(His admission creates a kind of opening between them. EDMOND *fills it by finishing tying his shoelaces, preparatory to leaving.)*

SHEILA: Having said that does not mean you have to run out.

EDMOND: What was I before you asked me to come here and help? Was I just some idiot spouting God?

SHEILA: No. I liked your sermons, actually. They were charming.

EDMOND: Yes. Well. Bullshit. Forgive me. Who was I talking to? They hold my hand now in a different way over in the nursing home. Its as if I know how to be there—just to—make a connection. Before, they were "souls", that's all. Interchangeable. Now I look into their eyes , and its hard to tear myself away. But how do you take that feeling and go back to being a priest?

SHEILA: *(To his extreme resistance to just staying and revealing himself this way:)* What? Edmond—it's all right. To reveal yourself isn't cause to go and hide under a rock.

EDMOND: I feel silly. Its just like this—*dense*—human being making contact with everyday life for the first time, and thinking—well, that its *good. (Beat)* What is it? Does what I just said sound stupid?

SHEILA: No. No. Edmond.

EDMOND: Then what?

SHEILA: I've been hoping you could get to this place, so that I can tell you.

EDMOND: Tell me what?

SHEILA: Those premonitions I've been having, that we are near the end? I've been seeing things in him more often. Slightly less life in the blind eyes, a new tone in the skin. I am afraid, Edmond.

EDMOND: But they're just premonitions.

SHEILA: Maybe.

EDMOND: Do you take this up with his doctors? You can't simply allow him to die.

SHEILA: Actually, I can. Edmond, that is what he is doing, and my job is to help him. *(Seeing that he still doesn't understand:)* The thing is, if it happens, when it happens, it's going to be difficult. I hate right now the fact of waiting for it to happen and being alone. I was thinking of asking you to stay. On the couch. Don't give me that deer-in-the-headlights look. On the couch. As a friend. A huge favor, I know

(Beat. Offering him the chance to surprise her, which he doesn't.)

EDMOND: Well I can't. Of course I can't. This is exactly what I'm talking about. I'm not supposed to be doing this hands—on. I'm supposed to be giving you a creed. Something to see you through whatever happens.

SHEILA: A "creed"? Lovely then. Give it to me, this creed. Remind me what it is, exactly, that we are to call to mind when a child dies in the night? What exactly did Jesus have to say on that subject, Father? Did he have a child? I seem to have forgotten. Tell me those words that make it unnecessary to have another person

touch you, in the middle of the night, when you lose
your child.

EDMOND: I have a priest coming in the morning.
A visitor from Ireland.

SHEILA: You didn't answer my question.

EDMOND: He won't die. There's—all kinds of life in him.

SHEILA: Yes. He's a bouncing boy.

EDMOND: If anything were to happen, you could call
me.

SHEILA: Yes. Yes I could, Father. And you'd be here
right away.

EDMOND: *(Seems to be considering)* No, I can't.

SHEILA: *(As he is on his way out)* Leave me a cross,
why don't you, Father? By the door. Or a creed.

EDMOND: Good night.

*(He exits. She retreats, pours herself more wine, finds another
C D. After a short while,* EDMOND *re-enters.* EDMOND *just
stands there at first, desperately uncertain about how to put
into words the thing he's come back to say.)*

SHEILA: You don't have to explain yourself to me. I
understand.

EDMOND: I'll tell you something. When he does—
when he does die. Not tonight, but when it happens,
you're going to want something more than *touch*.
You're going to want to believe there is something more
than this human *mess*, this human *pigsty*. You are going
to want the structure that only the Church represents.

SHEILA: We're on to structure now, are we? A minute
ago, you didn't want to go back to being that kind of
priest.

EDMOND: But suppose someone else needs me.

SHEILA: Oh, there's been a lot of that, hasn't there?
A lot of requests for your time.

EDMOND: But suppose someone did. And I wasn't
there—This is an indulgence for me, Sheila. I'm
supposed to be praying for you. My job is to support
the idea that the Church exists to absorb our pain.
That my solitude, my prayer, *absorbs* pain—

(Beat. They look at each other.)

SHEILA: Well, that's quite a speech. But it implies, of
course, that you *can* pray. But you've made your point.
Don't stay.

EDMOND: Is he dying?

SHEILA: I think so.

EDMOND: *(Beat)* Just when I've gotten to know him?

SHEILA: How God works, I think. Gives, and then takes
away.

EDMOND: Stop. Don't give me your easy criticism of
God. Any idiot can make that criticism. My life isn't
perfect, therefore there must not be a God. As if that
would be His plan, ever.
    Perfection for everybody.

SHEILA: Allright. I won't criticize your God.

EDMOND: Could it be tonight?

SHEILA: I don't know.

(Devastated, EDMOND *sits.)*

EDMOND: *(After a moment of being inside himself, almost
apologetically:)* How do you do it? *(Having a hard time
putting his thoughts together)* I think about you. I want
to scream at God sometimes. I want to make those
same stupid criticisms. I do. All those old people in
the nursing home, day after day, they live on.
    Why not them? Why not take one of them? This boy,

this child. I don't think priests were meant to feel,
Sheila. We did not come equipped to step out of the
priest's role into this—
    This, whatever this is—

*(After a moment of not looking at her, he reaches out
his hand. And after a moment's hesitation, she takes it.
But then he pulls his hand back and looks at it)*

SHEILA: What? Edmond?

*(They stand there just a moment in that fraught posture
before there is a knock on the door.* GARY *is there, a little
drunk.)*

GARY: Sheila.

SHEILA: *(Quietly but firmly, to* EDMOND*)* I'll get rid of
him. *(She goes to the door, remains just inside, not letting
him in)* What is it?

GARY: What's he still doing here?

SHEILA: What are you doing here, is more the question.

GARY: I didn't want to wait. I didn't want to wait to be
called.

SHEILA: I don't always call.

(SHEILA *goes "out", so that they are completely out of*
EDMOND's *view.)*

GARY: What is this? Its like clockwork. I sit at the bar.
The phone rings. Twelve-fifteen. Twelve-thirty.
    The bartender doesn't even say hello. Hands it right
to me.

SHEILA: But not tonight.

GARY: No. Not tonight. Why? *(He tries to look past her
into the house.)* He's *staying* with you? Going against
his *vows*? Jesus Christ, what are you trying to do?

SHEILA: Nothing. I wanted him to stay.

GARY: Improve your lot. Trade up.

SHEILA: Gary.

GARY: A step up from me.

SHEILA: What has been between us has always been—

GARY: What?

SHEILA: Has never been— *(Beat)* Serious.

GARY: *(Touches his own heart)* Oh, break my fucking
heart, why don't you? I thought it was.

SHEILA: You never thought it was.

GARY: *(The slightest mocking of her in his tone)* You won't
allow me *feeling*, will you? I'm not complex enough
for that? I'm some joke to you. The guy you call when
you're desperate enough, which is pretty regular lately.

SHEILA: Gary.

GARY: Suppose I wanted to go in there and tell him
what he walked into.

SHEILA: You wouldn't do that.

GARY: No? What I might do, though, is I might quit on
you.

(She looks at him. No immediate response, but a new tension.)

GARY: How's that? You find somebody on this island to
replace me, good luck.

SHEILA: You wouldn't do that.

GARY: I would miss Riley for sure. But I will not
be—*insulted*—this way. Why is he here?

SHEILA: *(Beat)* He comforts me.

GARY: And I don't.

SHEILA: What we've had has been a kind of comfort.
But not enough. I need more.

GARY: Ah. What, exactly? Spiritual comfort?

SHEILA: Don't make fun of me.

GARY: How long before he's in your bed?

SHEILA: *(Beat)* It is not that. Don't make it that.

GARY: *(Beat)* What story are you telling yourself, Sheila?

(She turns away.)

GARY: Alright. You're on your own. This is my notice.
(He starts to walk away.)

SHEILA: Gary.

(He turns.)

SHEILA: Don't do this. I need the help.

GARY: You should have thought more about that before you invited him to stay. If you need the help, you treat the help well.

SHEILA: Gary, he's dying.

GARY: Is he? You think you're gonna hold me that way? You think you're gonna make your world perfect that way?

(He exits. After a moment, SHEILA goes "in". EDMOND has slipped out; he's gone.)

SHEILA: Edmond?

(Cross-fade to:)

Scene Four

(The Monastery Garden)

(BOB, as he was in ACT ONE, *Scene Two: his hat, his hoe. This scene follows that earlier scene sequentially. It is perhaps a half hour later. Two chairs have been set up.* BOB *and* EDMOND *are seated. The sun)*

(On screen: trees)

BOB: So. This is where it stands. And you've come to me for—what, precisely? I'm unclear.

Empathy? Approval? Me, the self-punished apostle of passion?

EDMOND: Something simpler, Father. Advice.

BOB: Well, that is simple. Don't see her anymore. Preach to her from the pulpit, offer to take her son to his doctor's appointments, but stop this foolishness.

EDMOND: Is it foolishness, Father? Sometimes I feel like in not taking this burden from her I am a hypocrite to my faith.

BOB: Oh, please. Spending the night with her is being true to your faith? Which faith might that be, Edmond? You do know where this is likely to lead.

EDMOND: Father, I am not such an idiot as that. I don't want or need the sex.

BOB: Edmond, be honest.

EDMOND: I want to stop it here.

BOB: Because there is something to stop.

EDMOND: *(As much of an admission as he can muster)* When I would confess to you—as a seminarian—this was the last thing I ever thought would get in my way.

BOB: Don't torment yourself. It gets in the way. It has to be met.

EDMOND: Is that what—forgive me—is that what landed you here?

BOB: Well, aren't we bold.

(To EDMOND's *obvious chagrin at having asked this:)*

BOB: Edmond, it is a legitimate question. But tell me first. What's been going around?

EDMOND: Rumors.

*(*BOB *gestures for him to continue.)*

EDMOND: You and an—. *(He has another of his moments of selective aphasia.)*

BOB: "Altar boy"? Is that the abstract noun you're searching for? *(Beat. Considering a moment)* Very well. I'll tell you, Edmond. I used to do a foolish thing. I used to invite altar servers up to my house on the water in Camden, the one my parents left me. I never felt there was any particular danger in watching altar boys frolic in the water. It gave me—and them—pleasure. *(Beat)* Twenty years ago, there was one in particular. From out of the blue, in the middle of a summer day, volleyball on the lawn, boys in the water, I found myself looking at this one boy—a perfectly ordinary boy, I might add—and something very strange happened. I began to develop an obsession with this perfectly ordinary looking boy that I soon came to see was—well, almost *willed.* As though all those years of being a good priest, of holding things in, wanted at last to give way to something else. I couldn't take my eyes off him, at the beach, at mass, in the sacristy. All the while being aware there was nothing extraordinary to look at.

(Beat)

EDMOND: What happened?

BOB: I prayed. I thought, well, he'll grow up. *I'll grow up. This will pass. What is this? This is nothing. Hold on, I thought. Merely, hold on.* But that sort of self-coaching will only get you so far, Edmond. I began, after a time, to convince myself he was returning my stares. And one day, when all the altar servers had come charging down the stairs in their bathing suits and were headed toward the water, I realized he was not with them. He was still upstairs. I let them all go until the house was empty. I started up the stairs. *(Puts his hands over his heart)* Thump-a, thump-a, I assure you. To the top of the stairs. To find him, naked, or near enough, changing in the large room. And I looked at him. Our eyes met. *(Beat)* Holderlin. German poet. Said we're wrong about Paradise, Edmond. Its not some airy other region. Its here. An unseen world exists right before us at every moment of our lives. We cross to it on bridges lightly built, said Holderlin. Well, there on that upstairs landing was my bridge. We stared into each others eyes. For seconds, I think. To this day, I don't know what he was thinking, whether his eyes were filled with fear or intuition or else a terrible knowledge of me. I only know I did not cross, finally. I went back down the stairs, I returned to my priestly duties, and twenty years passed. Until one day, I received a call from the Bishop. This young man, in his mid-thirties now, had been haunted all these years by his encounter with me. A charge was made.

EDMOND: And you didn't refute it?

BOB: And say what? Well, yes, of course, I could have fought it, but not without telling terrible lies. *(Beat)* Well, there it is. And you must hear my stomach grumbling now. *(He makes to leave.)* You'll join me.

EDMOND: I'm not hungry.

BOB: Ah.

EDMOND: No, I'll go back early.

BOB: *(Clearly disappointed)* Such a long journey, for so little time.

EDMOND: *(Interrupting on "time")* Do you ever wonder now whether it wouldn't have been better to have crossed that bridge?

BOB: I could hardly be alive and not think that. In the end, I miss parish life—the very ordinariness of it— more than I miss any potential ecstasy I may have given up. They go, Edmond. Those desires go. *(Revising; out of an inherent honesty with himself)* Well, perhaps that's not quite true. Nonetheless. Come. We've harvested a crop of beets. I believe it's beet soup today.

(He starts off, then turns. He and EDMOND stare at one another a moment. Then EDMOND follows, before crossing to:)

Scene Five

(The Church)

(EDMOND begins preparing the altar for the next morning's Mass. It is evening.)

(SHEILA appears. She watches him. After awhile, he becomes aware of being watched, turns to her. He is surprised.)

EDMOND: I thought I was alone.

SHEILA: *(Beat)* I saw the lights. You keep it open at night now.

EDMOND: I've been advised against it. Vandals. But now that I'm here, mostly, nights, I keep an eye. Who's with Riley?

SHEILA: I hired a babysitter. I taught her the protocols. Don't worry. *(She checks her watch.)* One hour.

(Then, because there's an unmistakable look on his face:)

SHEILA: What's the question?

EDMOND: Hmm?

SHEILA: Does he miss you, perhaps?

EDMOND: *(Beat)* Does he?

SHEILA: I have no idea whether Riley misses you, but I find I do, Father.

(To his evasive response:)

SHEILA: Did you stop coming because Gary showed up that night?

EDMOND: You lied to me about him.

SHEILA: Not a lie. A sin of omission.

EDMOND: Why?

SHEILA: Could you have taken it? The ridiculous, the awful complexity of a life, of any life?

EDMOND: Gary's gone, then? You're doing it entirely by yourself?

SHEILA: I have taken a leave of absence from work until I can find someone. *(Light, not at all melodramatic about this:)* Some days I wonder if I am going to make it at all. Still—in the middle of those days, alone with him. Sometimes—well, I find I am immersed in a way I have always been frightened of being. I find its possible to give up—me. All my petty little— *(Waits for something from him)* Well, I'm surprised at myself. My capacity for selflessness.

EDMOND: Sheila, how much training did you give this babysitter?

SHEILA: I didn't?

EDMOND: *(Alarmed)* None at all? *(He seems about to take off.)*

SHEILA: *(Firm. Holding him with the power of her voice alone.)* Edmond. I take time away from him. Minutes. Just minutes. I need to.

EDMOND: You said an hour.

SHEILA: I said an hour, yes. *(She kneels down to pray.)*

EDMOND: *(Starting to go)* Maybe I should go and look after him.

SHEILA: Well, then you might, God forbid, feel again, Father, and wouldn't that be too difficult?

(Beat. Having gained his attention:)

SHEILA: I have been trying to make that thing happen that you talked about once. That end-of-the-day rush. In prayer. You remember?

EDMOND: Yes.

SHEILA: You can't *make* it happen, can you?

EDMOND: Sheila, if the babysitter doesn't know the protocols, and something *(Were to-)*

SHEILA: *(Overlapping)* Forget Riley for a moment. It's me who needs your help. Isn't that why I came to you at the beginning?

EDMOND: I never knew exactly why you came.

SHEILA: No? Well, imagine it, why don't you? Reach into that stunted place where Edmond lives and *imagine*—what my life was, my job and my nights with Riley, and then Gary would come and we'd have sex. And it was not in any way bad except that I had contempt for it. So there I was, this woman who cursed God and then went to church to curse God some more, and there, suddenly, you were—this interesting man, this soft—man. And I thought, I couldn't help but think—get him into your life. But then I seem to have found myself asking too much. *(She looks at him. As if she's catching him at something:)* You're doing it again.

EDMOND: What?

SHEILA: What you used to do at the beginning. Not looking at me. What is that?

EDMOND: It's called Custody of the Eyes. It's a practice. You do not look directly into the face of what can tempt you.

SHEILA: Oh, delicious. And were you tempted? That's what I'd like to know. Are you still—tempted?

(He avoids the question.)

SHEILA: You don't have to answer. *(She starts to go.)*

EDMOND: *(Screwing up his courage to say what he needs to:)* What right did you have to come into this church and—dig into my life—this way— So that it becomes meaningless. Can I ask that? I sit here, and I know I am doing everything that is right for a priest to do, and it feels like *shit*.

SHEILA: Such eloquence, Edmond.

EDMOND: Don't. You're smarter than me. You're always one step ahead of me. But you made me—*feel* things I have no right to feel. That people—that you and he—are more important than God. I have no right to feel that. It was given to me to take another stand.

SHEILA: Custody of the eyes. Wonderful. Know what I think? I think you looked at Riley, and at me, and saw something you had always wanted, but were afraid to grab. There it was. Right in front of you. You can have your prayer and your rush at the end of the day, but I think you will always know you missed something.

EDMOND: I think you make things up, Sheila. I think—I have no way to judge sanity, I don't know enough

about the world, but I think there was never—a fear
that you would drive into the water with him. I think
you did that to get me closer.

SHEILA: Amazing. You're doubting my sanity now.

EDMOND: And you are making this up. His death. That
he is so close to—his death. It was to get me to stay in
your house. And from there it was one step to—

SHEILA: Bed.

EDMOND: One step.

SHEILA: Oh, such a perceptive man. Would it stun you
to know that all I ever wanted was for you to hold me?

EDMOND: I don't believe that.

SHEILA: To put your arms around me.

EDMOND: No.

SHEILA: Still. I want that still. *(Beat)* Edmond. There is
no babysitter. I left him alone.

EDMOND: No.

SHEILA: He will not die tonight.

EDMOND: *(Making as though he's ready to go to* RILEY*)*
No? And if he does, whose fault will that be?

SHEILA: You have no right to step in now.

EDMOND: I think you have taken on too much. Sheila,
you can't do this alone. I am going to call in some help.

SHEILA: He will not die tonight. You may think I'm
insane but I know things. Wouldn't you like to know
things, Father? Wouldn't you like just once to have
gone so deep that you know somebody that well?

*(EDMOND is feeling, for the last time, the tremendous urge
toward her. He fights it.)*

SHEILA: I'm going back now. No need. We have no
need for you now. *(She looks at him a moment, goes.)*

(After another long moment of looking after her,
EDMOND *crosses to the rectory.)*

(Cross-fade to:)

Scene Six

(The cemetery)

*(The monks' garden—*BOB's *plot of earth—has been
transformed to a grave site. A single headstone.)*

*(*DON *and* BOB. DON *approaches the headstone. Reads the
names to himself. Wets his thumb and clears something that
has attached to the names. Steps back. Makes the sign of the
cross. Says a prayer. Then glances back at* BOB, *who is not
praying.)*

DON: None for you?

*(*BOB *prays, more to placate* DON *than out of his own
impulse.)*

DON: So he—?

BOB: Yes?

DON: Actually called? What? Social services?

BOB: Yes.

DON: And they—?

BOB: He proved negligence.

DON: Took the boy away. *(Beat)* And there he died.
In an institution. After—?

BOB: Two days.

DON: And so the question becomes— *(But another
question occurs to him)* They can just take them?

BOB: It was to be temporary. A warning, that's all.
The reflux alone, unattended to, could have killed
him at any moment.

DON: So the child knew her?

BOB: Apparently. Knew things had changed for him,
at any rate.

DON: And if he had not been—taken, would he have
died anyway? That's the question. And her journey
completed? *(Beat)* Ever read *The Bridge of San Luis Rey*?

BOB: No. No, my education, Donald, took place in the
twentieth century.

DON: Oh don't. Please. Wonderful book. Thornton
Wilder. Five people—five? —fell from a bridge. Why?
Why? And in each case God had a reason. And here,
she lets go of all support, as if she knew—*knew* it was
the end—and wanted the totality of the experience—
to carry someone to death—and its taken from her.
At the last moment. She does not get to watch him close
his eyes. To hold him. *(Beat)* Do we think we have any
grasp at all of human emotion?

BOB: We?

DON: Yes. Priests

BOB: Oh. Clearly not.

DON: *(He steps back.)* All we have to do sometimes is
hold still. Do nothing. Pascal. Remember? Our inability
to sit alone in a room the cause of all human misery.
Our job is so simple. To stand between them and terror.
Why can't we simply do it?

(They look at each other, then DON *returns to considering
the graves.)*

(Cross fade to:)

Scene Seven

(The Ferry)

*(*SHEILA*, in her car. Alone. Waiting. She punches in music. Crimson and Clover by Tommy James & the Shondells. Listens a moment, then turns it down. Looks once into the backseat, which is empty.then back to the front rather quickly.)*

(After a while, FERRYMAN *comes on. Stands at his perch, then looks back into* SHEILA's *car.)*

FERRYMAN: Where's the kid today?

*(*SHEILA *smiles weakly in response.)*

(A phone rings.)

(Lights up on rectory. Lights continue up on SHEILA *and the ferry area through the rest of the play.* MRS CALLAHAN *comes on and answers phone.)*

MRS CALLAHAN: Yes? Yes, he's—he's here. He's— *(Beat. A great pained look. She puts the phone down, calls off:)* Father?

EDMOND: *(Off)* What is it, Mrs Callahan?

MRS CALLAHAN: Phone for you, Father. It's the ferry service. Something's happened. *(She goes off, carrying phone.)*

(Lights down on Rectory, up on the ferry area behind SHEILA *and the* FERRYMAN. Crimson & Clover *continues to play. We do not lose* SHEILA. *But we are back on the ferry, too.* DON *and* BOB *enter the ferry, having had to run to make this boat, carrying their luggage.)*

DON: Well, there it is. There's my excursion. The scandal tucked away. Pot roast eaten. Parishioners

smiled at. But something I'd still like to know.
Where did he go, do you suppose?

BOB: I suspect he followed an old example.
Became a wanderer. A hermit.

DON: Saint Jerome.

BOB: In a cave somewhere.

DON: No. Somewhere else. We must find him.
I'd like to talk with him.

BOB: *(Beat)* When will you be making your decision,
Bishop, about the church.

DON: *(Beat)* I'm going to close it down, Robert.
There's a perfectly good church on the mainland.
Bill Montrechard's parish. If four hundred and
seventy-three people—excuse me, a *third* of that—
most of them had to take the ferry anyway—they
can take it this way. No harm. *(Beat)* I'm afraid I have
no man to send there. I'm sorry to disappoint you.
You had your heart set, I imagine. The cozy parish.
Mrs Callahan bringing you tea while you touch up the
notes for your sermon by the fire. That Church is dead.
There will be fewer and fewer of us, and people will
have to travel farther and farther, but forgive me, I can't
feel that's altogether a bad thing. Let it shrink. This is
no tragedy. Our Lord doesn't want that ease for us,
Father. "I come not to bring you peace but a sword".
Something before us we want, and He snatches it
away and says no, something else. I want—for you—
something else.

FERRYMAN: *(Glancing at SHEILA)* Ferry coming.
(He removes the rope)

*(EDMOND comes on. He examines his hand, as though he
is overcoming a long struggle. He is not looking at SHEILA,
but addressing the audience, as he did at the beginning.)*

EDMOND: The nun, wasn't exaggerating really. She was telling the truth. Something is handed to us. Could you love this baby as you love me? *(He raises his hand, with great difficulty.)*

(Lights down.)

END OF PLAY